FIGHTING FORCES OF WORLD WAR II

AT
SEA

John C. Miles

CAPSTONE PRESS
a capstone imprint

Edge Books are published by Capstone Press
1710 Roe Crest Drive, North Mankato, Minnesota 56003
www.mycapstone.com

Library of Congress Cataloging-in-Publication Data
Names: Miles, John C. (John Christian), 1960– author.
Title: Fighting forces of World War II at sea / by John C. Miles.
Description: North Mankato, Minnesota : Capstone Press, [2020] | Series: Edge
books. Fighting forces of World War II | Includes bibliographical
references and index. | Audience: Grades 4-6. | Audience: Ages 8–12.
Identifiers: LCCN 2018060642 | ISBN 9781543574814 (hardcover)
Subjects: LCSH: World War, 1939–1945—Naval operations—Juvenile literature.
| Warships—History—20th century—Juvenile literature. | Submarines
(Ships)—History—20th century—Juvenile literature. |
Navies—History—20th century—Juvenile literature.
Classification: LCC D770 .M46 2020 | DDC 940.54/5—dc23
LC record available at https://lccn.loc.gov/2018060642

Summary: Explores the ships and submarines that battled for
control of the seas during World War II, and provides information
about key battles, tactics, and weapons that helped propel the Allies to victory.

Editorial Credits
Editor: Julia Bird
Series designer: John Christopher/White Design
Photo researcher: Diana Morris

Photo Credits
Admiralty Official Collection/IWM: 13b. alexandarilich/Shutterstock: 28t. AP/Topfoto: 10bl. Lt. R G G
Coote/IWM: 14bl. Crown ©/Wikimedia Commons: 22t. Everett Historical/Shutterstock: front cover t, b,
back cover, 1, 4bl, 4tr, 5t, 26b. Flanker/CC Wikimedia Commons: 16tl. Jeffrey M Frank/Shutterstock: 10br.
The Granger Collection, NY/Topfoto: 13t, 25b. Haifa Museum/CC Wikimedia Commons: 17t. IWM: 8t,
18b, 23t. Ken/CC Wikimedia Commons: 6t. Keystone/Getty Images: 27b. Carlo Maggio/Alamy: 16b. MOI/
IWM: 12c. MOI/Polish official photographer/IWM: 19t. National Archives/CC Wikimedia Commons: 15tl.
National Navy UDT-SEAL Museum: 24bl, 24bc. David Newton/CC Wikimedia Commons: 14tl. Pathé/
Topfoto: 7b. PD/Wikimedia Commons: 20b, 27c, 29c. Picturepoint/Topfoto: 12b. Popperfoto/Getty
Images: 11b, 28b. Frank Scherschel/The LIFE Picture Collection/Getty Images: 15b. Lt. H.W. Tomlin/IWM:
8b. Topfoto: 5b, 6b, 9c, 9b, 11t, 17c, 19b, 21, 23b. Alex Tora/CC Wikimedia Commons: 20t. Sgt Turner,
No 1 Army Film & Photographic Unit/IWM: 22c. Ullsteinbild/Topfoto: 6c, 7t, 17b. U.S. Navy photograph/
PD/Wikimedia Commons: 20c, 24tl, 26t, 27t. Vilegecko/CC Wikimedia Commons: 12t. CC Wikimedia
Commons: 10tl, 15tr, 18tl. E.A. Zimmerman/Royal Navy official photographer/IWM: 29t.

All internet sites appearing in back matter were available
and accurate when this book was sent to press.

First published in Great Britain in 2018
by The Watts Publishing Group
Copyright © The Watts Publishing Group, 2018

This book is dedicated to the memory of Vice-Admiral Sir Peter Berger RN (1925-2003), who served on
HMS *Ajax* during the Second World War.

Printed and bound in China
1593

Table of Contents

War Begins 4

German U-Boats 6

The Merchant Navy 8

Convoy Escorts 10

Battleship *Bismarck* 12

Free French Naval Forces 14

The Regia Marina and 10th Assault Flotilla 16

Royal Marine Commandos 18

The Imperial Japanese Navy 20

The Special Boat Section 22

U.S. Navy Combat Demolition Teams.................. 24

The U.S. Pacific Fleet 26

X-Class Midget Submarines...................................... 28

Glossary and Timeline.. 30

Read More and Internet Sites................................... 31

Index.. 32

War Begins

In 1918 Germany lost World War I (1914–1918) and was forced to sign the Treaty of Versailles. Its harsh terms were very unpopular with Germans. In 1933 they elected a new leader, Adolf Hitler, who promised to restore Germany's standing in the world.

Hitler rides through cheering crowds in the German city of Kassel in 1939.

Rise of the Nazis

Hitler's Nazi (National Socialist) Party believed that their country should rule over all others and that certain groups of people, such as Jews, were trying to cheat Germany. Under the Nazis, Germany began to build up its armed forces and take over land in nearby countries. Finally, on September 1, 1939, German forces invaded neighboring Poland.

Allied Forces and Axis Powers

Britain and the countries of its empire and dominions, such as Canada and Australia, joined France to declare war on Germany. These countries became known as the Allied forces. During 1940 Hitler took control of Denmark, Norway, France, Belgium, and the Netherlands. Italy joined the war on the side of the Nazis, forming the Axis powers. They were later bolstered by Japan. In June 1941 Germany invaded the Soviet Union. Then in December, Japan attacked a U.S. naval base, bringing the might of the United States into World War II (1939–1945).

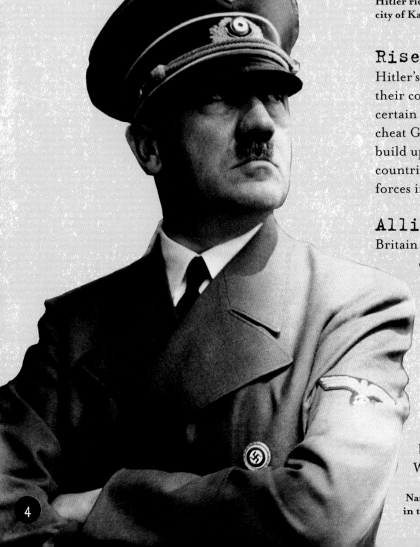

Nazi dictator Adolf Hitler, pictured in the late 1930s.

The War Turns

Throughout 1942 and 1943, Allied and Axis forces battled in North Africa, Italy, the Soviet Union, and the Pacific as the war went global. Italy surrendered in September 1943. In June 1944 Allied forces launched Operation Overlord to begin taking back Europe. Months of fighting followed before the Allies began to advance toward Germany, something that the Soviet Union had begun to do from the east. Crushed in a massive pincer movement, Nazi forces were defeated. Hitler committed suicide at the end of April 1945 as Germany's capital, Berlin, fell to the Allies.

The Atomic Bomb

In the Pacific the war had raged on. To end it, President Harry Truman authorized the use of the most terrible weapon ever invented—the atomic bomb—which obliterated the Japanese cities of Hiroshima and Nagasaki in August 1945. Japan finally surrendered. World War II was over.

The atomic "mushroom cloud" rises above Nagasaki, Japan.

A TERRIBLE TOLL

The cost of the war in human lives was staggering. Historians estimate that more than 21-25 million soldiers and up to 55 million civilians were killed. Around 6 million were Jews who were murdered by the Nazis during the Holocaust.

World War II at Sea

Naval forces fought around the world during World War II, from the North Atlantic, where the Allies battled German submarines, to the South Pacific, where the U.S. Navy and Australian and New Zealand forces fought the Imperial Japanese Navy. At the beginning of the war, Great Britain's Royal Navy was the largest and most powerful in the world. By the end of the war, the U.S. Navy had expanded massively to become the world's biggest. This book looks at just some of the naval forces that fought during the war.

Torpedoed by a Nazi U-boat, a merchant ship sinks during the Battle of the Atlantic.

GERMAN U-BOATS

	ACTIVE:	STRENGTH:
	1939-45	1,140 vessels (1939-45)
	AREAS ACTIVE: North Atlantic, North Sea, South Atlantic	

Within hours of the beginning of World War II, in September 1939, Nazi U-boats, or submarines, began attacking Allied ships. Thus began the Battle of the Atlantic—the longest campaign of the war.

Scapa Flow

U-boats were to prove Germany's most effective weapon in the war at sea, attacking Allied warships as well as merchant shipping. In October 1939 Captain Günther Prien managed to steer his submarine *U-47* undetected into the Royal Navy's base at Scapa Flow in Orkney off the northern coast of Scotland. There he torpedoed and sank the British battleship HMS *Royal Oak*. This action shocked the British, who had considered the base to be invincible. Prien returned to a hero's welcome in Germany. Under Prien's command, *U-47* sank more than 30 Allied ships before it was in turn sunk in 1941.

U-boat Captain Günther Prien (directly below flag) and crew

HMS *Royal Oak*, which was sunk by *U-47*. More than 800 crew members died in the attack. The wreck of the ship lies under 100 feet (30 meters) of water and is a protected war grave.

German shipyard workers launch a type VIIC U-boat in 1941.

TYPE VII U-BOAT

- **SPEED** 20 miles (32 kilometers) per hour surfaced; 8.6 miles (14 km) per hour submerged
- **RANGE** 9,750 miles (15,700 km) surfaced; 93 miles (150 km) submerged

The type VII was the most common Nazi U-boat. It was armed with quick-firing deck guns, antiaircraft guns, and up to 14 torpedoes. Carrying 44-52 crew members, the type VII traveled on the surface most of the time, where its diesel engines powered it along. When the ship submerged to attack or escape, the type VII used electric motors powered by batteries.

HMS *Barham*

In November 1941 the Royal Navy battleship HMS *Barham* was cruising off the coast of Egypt when it was intercepted by U-boat *U-331*. Hit by three torpedoes at close range, *Barham* didn't stand a chance—a gigantic explosion blew the vessel apart, killing 862 men. The sinking (below) was captured by a news cameraman on board a nearby ship and remains a lasting record of the devastation wrought by a single U-boat attack.

Starting in 1942, new antisubmarine weapons and tactics, plus the entry of the United States into the war, meant that the Allies were gradually able to win the battle against the German U-boats.

WHO'S WHO AT SEA IN WORLD WAR II

Many types of warships fought at sea during World War II:

- Battleships and battle cruisers, armed with huge naval guns, were a navy's biggest ships. Below them were cruisers.

- Aircraft carriers acted as floating airbases and allowed naval planes to strike at the enemy from the sea.

- Fast-moving destroyers and corvettes had smaller guns, as well as torpedoes. They acted as escorts for bigger ships and played a key role in antisubmarine warfare.

- Much smaller vessels, such as landing craft, delivered troops and tanks to a beach for a seaborne invasion.

Hit in the middle, HMS *Barham* was ripped apart by a huge explosion. Amazingly, there were 487 survivors.

THE MERCHANT NAVY

ACTIVE: 1939-45	STRENGTH: 185,000
AREAS ACTIVE: Atlantic Ocean, Arctic Ocean	

Throughout the Battle of the Atlantic, the brave sailors of the Merchant Navy risked their lives to bring vital war supplies to Allied nations.

Essential Service

As an island nation, Great Britain depended heavily on imports, needing more than 1.1 million tons (1 million metric tons) of supplies per week just to allow it to survive and carry on the war. The only way to get this quantity of goods to Great Britain was by merchant ship. Nazi U-boat commanders were therefore ordered to sink as many Allied merchant ships as possible in a bid to cripple Great Britain's war effort.

Life on Board

Life on merchant ships was hard, and food and accommodation for sailors was basic. Sailors "signed on" for each voyage and did a variety of jobs, from ship-handling and navigation to shoveling coal into the ship's engines. The majority of seamen who crewed merchant ships were British. However there were also large numbers of sailors from India, China, the West Indies, Africa, Canada, and Australia.

Crew members aboard the convoy escort destroyer HMS *Vanoc* watch over a nearby merchant ship.

Convoys

Merchant ships sailed together in large groups called convoys. Assembling in a harbor—such as Halifax on Canada's eastern coast—ships set off on their voyages escorted by smaller warships, such as destroyers and corvettes. These ships provided some protection from Nazi U-boats, but once enemy submarines located a convoy in the vastness of the ocean the results could be devastating. In September 1940, convoy HX72, consisting of 42 ships, was attacked by four U-boats. Over two days the convoy lost 11 of its ships.

TORPEDOED!

Many merchant ships had light guns for self-defense, but once torpedoed a merchant ship had little chance of staying afloat. How quickly a ship sank depended on its cargo—if it was loaded with flammable aviation fuel there could be a huge explosion and few survivors. Ships carrying other goods sank more slowly, perhaps giving the crew time to launch lifeboats or swim to floating debris and await rescue by a nearby ship. Some U-boat crews even surfaced to pick up survivors. Nevertheless, thousands of sailors drowned in the freezing cold waters of the Atlantic.

Hit by a U-boat's torpedoes, an Allied merchant ship quickly sinks below the Atlantic's waves.

ARCTIC CONVOYS

From 1941 to 1945, around 1,400 merchant ships formed 78 convoys that sailed from Great Britain, Iceland, and North America to the Soviet Union, carrying key fighter planes, fuel, ammunition, and food. Escorted by warships of the Royal Navy, Royal Canadian Navy, and the U.S. Navy, these convoys sailed around German-occupied Norway, braving U-boats, extreme seas, and freezing Arctic weather that left the ships coated in thick ice.

Crew members aboard HMS *Vansittart* hack away at massive sheets of ice while on Arctic convoy duty in February 1943.

CONVOY ESCORTS

ACTIVE: 1940	STRENGTH: 294 ships
AREAS ACTIVE: North Atlantic, Arctic	

Throughout World War II, small warships braved rough seas and deadly U-boat "wolf packs" to escort convoys safely across the Atlantic.

Tribal-Class Destroyer

These 377-foot (115-m) long all-purpose warships were developed in the 1930s, and used by the Royal Navy, the Royal Canadian Navy, and the Royal Australian Navy. The ships were armed with eight 120-mm or 102-mm quick-firing naval guns and four 40-mm or 20-mm antiaircraft guns, as well as torpedo tubes and 20 antisubmarine depth charges. Able to speed along at 42 miles (67 km) per hour and operated by a crew of 200, these warships were among the most modern of World War II.

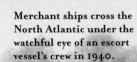

Merchant ships cross the North Atlantic under the watchful eye of an escort vessel's crew in 1940.

HMCS *HAIDA*

Only one Tribal-class destroyer, HMCS *Haida*, survives today. It is permanently moored in Hamilton, Ontario, Canada, as a museum ship. *Haida* and its sister ship, HMCS *Eskimo*, sank the German Type VII U-boat *U-971* in the English Channel on June 24, 1944.

Flower-Class Corvette

Below destroyers in size and firepower, but far more numerous, these light warships were mainly used as convoy protection vessels. They served with the Royal Navy, the Royal Canadian Navy, and the U.S. Navy, as well as the navies of Australia, New Zealand, and other countries. Flower-class corvettes were 206 feet (63 m) long and carried a crew of 90. They were armed with a single 102-mm naval gun, three antiaircraft guns, 70 depth charges, and other antisubmarine weapons.

Antisubmarine Weapons

Once a U-boat was detected, naval commanders attacked it with a range of weapons. Depth charges were underwater bombs set to explode at a certain depth. If one blew up near a U-boat, the underwater shock wave could split the submarine's hull, allowing water to rush in and sink it. "Hedgehog" or "Squid" antisubmarine bombs were fired over the bow of an attacking ship. These weapons had contact fuses, meaning they had to hit the submarine in order to explode. But they were much more effective than depth charges.

Royal Navy crew load a depth charge into a thrower.

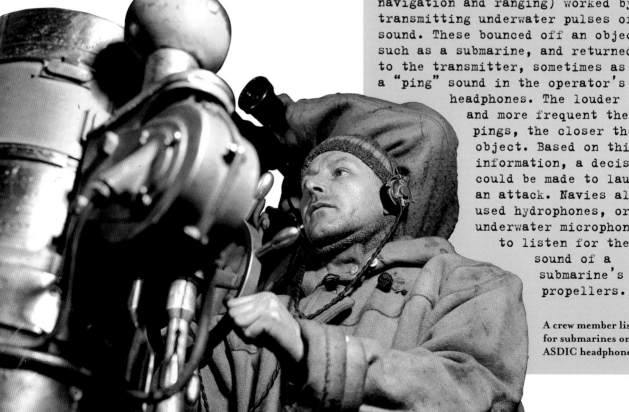

ASDIC AND SONAR

Initially developed during World War I, ASDIC (antisubmarine detection) and sonar (sound navigation and ranging) worked by transmitting underwater pulses of sound. These bounced off an object, such as a submarine, and returned to the transmitter, sometimes as a "ping" sound in the operator's headphones. The louder and more frequent the pings, the closer the object. Based on this information, a decision could be made to launch an attack. Navies also used hydrophones, or underwater microphones, to listen for the sound of a submarine's propellers.

A crew member listens for submarines on ASDIC headphones.

BATTLESHIP *BISMARCK*

	LAUNCHED: 1939	CREW STRENGTH: 2,200
	AREAS ACTIVE: North Sea, North Atlantic	

In 1941 a tense game of cat and mouse was played out in the North Atlantic, as the Royal Navy tried to locate and destroy one of Nazi Germany's most powerful warships.

The *Bismarck*

Launched in 1939, Germany's battleship *Bismarck* was a floating fortress. It was armed with eight huge 38-cm naval guns in four swiveling armored turrets, 44 smaller naval guns, and antiaircraft guns. German naval commanders intended to use the *Bismarck* to attack Allied merchant shipping in the North Atlantic. In 1941, the *Bismarck* was moved to Nazi-occupied Norway for safety and anchored in a narrow sea inlet with the cruiser *Prinz Eugen*.

The Royal Navy battle cruiser HMS *Hood*

Battle of the Denmark Strait

On May 21, 1941, *Bismarck* and *Prinz Eugen* left Norway and headed for the Atlantic. They were shadowed by a Royal Navy squadron, including the battle cruiser HMS *Hood*. On May 24 the two sides met in battle in the Denmark Strait, but after only ten minutes one of *Bismarck's* massive shells hit the middle of the *Hood*, exploding its main magazine. The *Hood* broke in two and sank in just three minutes, killing 1,415 men.

The *Bismarck* pictured firing its main battery of eight 38-cm guns.

Find the *Bismarck*!

The *Bismarck* had been damaged in the battle, so Admiral Günther Lütjens decided to head for the port of Saint-Nazaire in Nazi-occupied France, where repairs could be made. But the Royal Navy had other ideas and sent a massive task force to sink it.

A first attack by torpedo bomber planes scored one hit, but the *Bismarck* then managed to slip away. Eventually, however, British code breakers deciphered messages sent by the enemy. This, combined with the use of on-board radar, allowed the Royal Navy to figure out the *Bismarck*'s new position. A new wave of torpedo planes from HMS *Ark Royal* then moved in. One torpedo scored a direct hit on *Bismarck*'s port rudder, leaving the ship unable to steer as the British task force approached.

A British Fairey Swordfish bomber launches a torpedo.

Sinking

At daybreak on May 27 the business of sinking the *Bismarck* began, as shell after shell from battleships HMS *Rodney* and HMS *King George V* pounded the enemy. The *Bismarck* could not return fire accurately, but its remaining crew refused to surrender. By 10 a.m. the *Bismarck* was a smoking wreck but still afloat, protected by its thick hull armor. Eventually the *Bismarck*'s crew set off demolition charges to sink what remained of the ship as HMS *Dorsetshire* launched a torpedo attack. The *Bismarck* sank at 10:40 a.m. Out of its crew of 2,200, there were only 114 survivors.

RADAR

This technology was developed in great secrecy during the 1930s, and played a key part in World War II. Radar stands for "radio detection and ranging." In radar systems, a transmitter sends out pulses of radio waves, which bounce off an object, such as a ship, before returning to the system's receiver. The operator can then figure out how far away the object is and how fast it is traveling. Radar was key to Great Britain's victory in the Battle of Britain and was also used extensively in the war at sea.

Radar operators helped direct the ship's gunfire at the enemy.

ARMOR ON SHIPS

Warships were protected by hardened steel armor up to 14 inches (360 mm) thick. Armor was thickest on a ship's hull, gun turrets, and on the "citadel," which included the bridge from where the ship was commanded and steered. Most ships had thinner armor on their decks to save weight. As the loss of HMS *Hood* demonstrated, in the event of a direct hit this could be a critical weak spot.

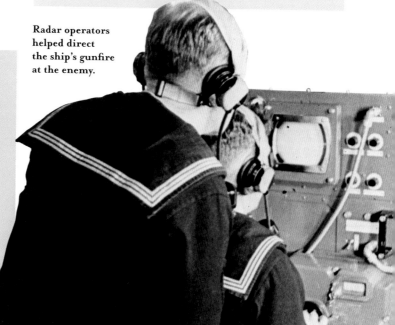

FREE FRENCH NAVAL FORCES

FORMED:
1940

AREAS ACTIVE:
Western Europe, Pacific

STRENGTH:
1 obsolete aircraft carrier, 2 battleships, 2 cruisers, 5 destroyers, 22 escort vessels, 9 submarines, numerous other small vessels

When France was invaded by Germany in June 1940, French naval forces had to choose whether to go along with the Nazi occupation of their country or to help fight it.

France Splits

French leader Philippe Pétain signed an armistice with the Nazis on June 22. This ended the fighting, but turned the northern part of France into a German occupation zone. The southern part of the country was controlled by a French government—the "Vichy" government—which was sympathetic to the Nazis.

De Gaulle's Appeal

French General Charles de Gaulle, who had escaped to London, made a famous radio speech in which he appealed to the French military and civilians everywhere to join his "Free French Forces" and continue the war by fighting with the Allies. Days after de Gaulle made this appeal, Admiral Émile Muselier joined de Gaulle. The crew of the submarine *Narval* also pledged support. This, plus the acquisition of a few ships—such as the destroyer *Léopard* that had been docked in British ports—meant that the Free French possessed the beginnings of a naval force.

General de Gaulle, leader of the Free French Forces, inspects officers and sailors on board the destroyer *Léopard*.

The Navy Grows

As the war progressed, the Free French fleet grew in size. It received a big boost in November 1942 when the territory of French West Africa, which had previously supported the Vichy regime, declared its support for de Gaulle. As a result, the Free French Navy acquired a modern battleship, the *Richelieu*, one heavy and three light cruisers, plus several destroyers, all of which had been stationed at the port of Dakar.

The heavy cruiser *Montcalm* had been stationed in Dakar.

JACQUES COUSTEAU

One of the most well-known members of the Free French naval forces was the diver and filmmaker Jacques Cousteau (1910–1997). He codeveloped the aqualung in the mid-1940s and took part in many commando operations during the war.

In Action

During the D-Day landings on June 6, 1944, 11 Free French ships took part in Operation Neptune, the naval action that supported Allied invasion forces. Heavy ships, such as the cruiser *Montcalm,* bombarded the Nazis with gunfire as troops swept onto the beaches of Normandy. Free French naval commandos also attacked German positions on the cliffs above the invasion beaches.

Some Free French ships, such as the destroyer *Triomphant,* served in the Pacific area, where its crew helped to evacuate civilians ahead of the invasion of Nauru in 1942. Later the ship helped to protect Australia from Japanese attack.

A battleship pounds Nazi defenses on D-Day, while landing craft prepare to deliver troops onto the beaches of Normandy.

THE REGIA MARINA AND 10TH ASSAULT FLOTILLA

FORMED:	STRENGTH:
1940	200 vessels
AREAS ACTIVE: Mediterranean	

Italy joined World War II on the Axis side after the fall of France. In the Mediterranean, the Italian Navy posed a very real threat to the might of Great Britain's Royal Navy.

The Regia Marina

At the beginning of the war the Italian Navy, or Regia Marina, looked like a formidable force. It had six battleships, 19 cruisers, 59 destroyers, and other vessels including torpedo boats and submarines. However, many Italian vessels were obsolete, lacking modern equipment such as radar. There were operational issues as well. In battle, Regia Marina commanders were required to seek approval from their bosses on shore before taking critical action. This often resulted in a missed opportunity to deal a decisive blow to the enemy.

War in the Mediterranean

During the early part of the war, the Royal Navy and the Regia Marina battled for control of the Mediterranean Sea. The Royal Navy's bases in Gibraltar, Malta, and Egypt were key to its ability to protect the Suez Canal and the sea route to British India—making them high-priority Axis targets.

Many Italian naval vessels, like this submarine, were out of date and unable to tackle the more modern equipment of the Royal Navy.

10th Assault Flotilla

This elite Italian naval special forces unit was created shortly after Italy entered the war. By the war's end, the unit had sunk more than 79,000 tons (72,000 metric tons) of Allied warships and more than 143,000 tons (130,000 metric tons) of merchant shipping. The 10th Flotilla used a range of innovative attack equipment, including MT assault boats and SLC torpedoes.

An MT assault boat

MT ASSAULT BOATS

- **CREW** 1
- **EXPLOSIVE CHARGE** 660 pounds (300 kilograms)

These small, fast motorboats were packed with explosives. Launched from a destroyer, the assault boat's operator would speed toward the target, then jump overboard before impact. On March 25, 1941, an MT squadron attacked British ships at Suda Bay on the island of Crete. The heavy cruiser HMS *York* was heavily damaged. The commandos also sank two oil tankers and a cargo ship.

SLC TORPEDOES

- **CREW** 2
- **EXPLOSIVE CHARGE** 660 pounds (300 kg)

The most famous weapon used by the 10th Flotilla was the SLC manned torpedo, nicknamed the *Maiale*, or "pig." On December 3, 1941, the Italian submarine *Sciré* delivered three *Maiale* to the harbor at Alexandria, Egypt, where the Royal Navy battleships HMS *Valiant* and *Queen Elizabeth* were at anchor. The mines they placed sank the two battleships, as well as a Norwegian tanker. The battleships sank in only a few feet of water and were later repaired, but the attack put them out of action for more than a year.

HMS *Queen Elizabeth* (center), and (right) two navy divers ride an SLC manned torpedo through a battleship's antitorpedo nets.

ROYAL MARINE COMMANDOS

FORMED:	STRENGTH
1940	6,000–8,000

AREAS ACTIVE:	
Western Europe, Asia	

Founded in 1940 and active throughout World War II, Royal Marine Commando units became famous for carrying out daring seaborne raids in enemy territory.

Origins

The Royal Marines were historically soldiers who fought with the Royal Navy. Founded by Prime Minister Winston Churchill, the first "Special Service Brigades"—later known as Commandos—included personnel from both the British Army and Royal Marines. Each Commando battalion contained about 450 men, organized into troops of 75 and subsections of 15. By 1942, 6,000 Royal Marines had volunteered for Commando units, and by the end of the war nine RM Commando battalions had been raised.

Commandos smile for the camera as they return from a daring mission to capture Nazi radar equipment in June 1942.

Tough Training

By 1942 Commando recruits trained in Scotland where, on arrival, they had to make an 8-mile (13-km) march from the railway station to their training camp while carrying all their equipment. Training focused on extreme physical fitness, and those who failed to make the grade were marked "RTU" or "return to unit." Commando training exercises used live ammunition and explosives to make conditions as real as possible, and the skills recruits learned included survival, river crossings, mountain climbing, and hand-to-hand combat.

Operations

RM Commando units conducted a range of daring operations against enemy forces during the course of World War II. In 1940 and 1941, Commandos supported Allied campaigns against German forces in occupied Norway, spearheading attacks on enemy positions and factories producing war supplies. In 1942 and 1943, Commando units took part in the landings in North Africa, Sicily, and Italy, and on June 6, 1944, Commandos went ashore on D-Day. Toward the end of the war, Commando units fought bravely against Japanese forces in Burma (now Myanmar).

Commandos in training, 1942

COCKLESHELL HEROES

In December 1942, 10 RM Commandos attacked ships carrying enemy war supplies in the harbor at Bordeaux, France. The men set off from a submarine in five two-man folding canoes known as Cockles. Two men drowned when their craft capsized. Another four were captured and shot by the Germans.

The remaining four Commandos eventually reached Bordeaux harbor by paddling under cover of darkness. They attached mines to the hulls of six ships, which exploded and caused severe damage. After the operation was complete, two more of the cockleshell heroes were captured and shot, while the final two escaped to safety in neutral Spain.

Two Commando raiders pictured with their "cockleshell" canoe.

THE IMPERIAL JAPANESE NAVY

ACTIVE: 1941–45	**STRENGTH (1941):** 10 battleships, 10 aircraft carriers, 38 cruisers, 112 destroyers, 65 submarines, support vessels
AREAS ACTIVE: Pacific	

The government that controlled Japan in the 1930s attempted to dominate the Pacific region, invading China in 1937 and attacking the United States in 1941. As an island nation, the might of the Imperial Japanese Navy (IJN) was key to the country's early military successes in World War II.

Preparing for War

Since the 1870s, Japan had been building up and modernizing its navy. As early as 1920, the Imperial Japanese Navy was the third biggest in the world, after Great Britain and the United States. By the late 1930s, Japan had scored several important naval firsts. It had launched the world's first aircraft carrier, the *Hōshō*, in 1921, had pioneered the use of very large guns on battleships, and had developed modern destroyers armed with advanced torpedoes. But the IJN lagged behind other nations in submarine warfare, technology such as radar, and secure communications.

The IJN aircraft carrier *Hōshō*

Aircraft aboard an IJN aircraft carrier prepare to attack Pearl Harbor on December 7, 1941.

Early Success and Defeat

Throughout 1941 and 1942, the armed forces of Japan steamrollered through the Pacific region, inflicting heavy defeats on the Allies. On December 10, 1941, Japanese naval aircraft sank two Royal Navy battleships, HMS *Repulse* and HMS *Prince of Wales*, in the South China Sea. In April 1942, the IJN attacked the Royal Navy in the Indian Ocean, making part of the force retreat to East Africa.

The Japanese Navy's seemingly unstoppable advance was eventually checked by a series of devastating defeats at the hands of the Allies, beginning at the Battle of Midway in June 1942. By 1943 the Allies, particularly the United States, were building new ships and replacing battle losses much faster than Japan, which was running short of war materials and combat-trained personnel.

YAMATO

- **SPEED** 31 miles (50 km) per hour
- **RANGE** 8,260 miles (13,300 km)

This monster ship and its sister ship, the *Mushashi*, were the biggest battleships ever built. Launched in 1940, the *Yamato* was 863 feet (263 m) long and armed with nine huge 46-cm naval guns, 12 15.5-cm guns, 12 127-mm guns, and 28 antiaircraft guns. It carried seven aircraft and had thick steel armor. In April 1945, as the Allies battled the Japanese for the island of Okinawa, *Yamato* was sent as part of a counterattack force but was instead attacked by waves of Allied air strikes. After 11 torpedo hits and more than six direct bomb hits, the huge ship rolled over, blew up, and sank, killing an estimated 3,055 crew members.

The battleship *Yamato* nears completion in a Japanese dockyard.

THE SPECIAL BOAT SECTION

	FORMED: 1940	STRENGTH: 100-250 approx.
	AREAS ACTIVE: Mediterranean, Asia	

Like the Royal Marine Commandos, the Special Boat Section (SBS) was founded in 1940 to conduct dangerous secret missions. Renamed the Special Boat Service after the war, today the unit is still part of the UK's Special Forces.

Eccentric Founder

The SBS was founded by Roger Courtney, a Commando. Courtney was convinced that a small naval force, operating from folding kayaks, could boost the war effort by conducting raids on enemy shipping. Courtney's first attempts to convince Royal Navy officials of the worth of his idea were unsuccessful. So, while in Scotland, Courtney paddled to a British warship, HMS *Glengyle*, anchored in the Clyde River. There he secretly climbed aboard and wrote his initials on the door to the captain's cabin before stealing a deck gun cover. Afterward Courtney went to a nearby hotel where a group of high-ranking Royal Navy officers were meeting and presented them with the cover. He was promoted to captain and given command of a new unit, the Special Boat Section.

A corporal of the SBS prepares his weapons for action.

Mediterranean Ops

The men of the SBS deployed to the Mediterranean in 1941, working with the 1st Submarine Flotilla, which delivered SBS men to their targets. The SBS undertook reconnaissance missions on enemy-occupied Greek islands and supported the evacuation of troops from Crete. A second unit, No. 2 SBS, was formed in December 1941.

Greek boats of the type that transported SBS members to their targets. The vessels were typically armed with one 50-mm cannon and two machine guns.

Airfield Raids

In June 1942, No. 1 SBS raided airfields on German-occupied Crete and, in September, Rhodes, which were being used by enemy aircraft to attack British convoys in the Mediterranean. In the Rhodes operation, code-named "Operation Anglo," the SBS managed to destroy numerous aircraft, a fuel dump, and some buildings, but only two men returned to the waiting submarine—the rest were captured and became prisoners of war.

Later Missions

After these operations, No. 1 SBS became part of the Special Air Service (SAS) and was renamed the Special Boat Squadron. They worked with Greek special forces and, in 1944, fought alongside the Allies in Greece and Italy. No. 2 SBS did vital reconnaissance work for U.S. forces in North Africa in November 1942. Then they supported Allied landings in Sicily, before being redeployed to the campaign against Japanese forces in Burma toward the end of the war.

MAJOR ANDERS LASSEN

One of the most famous SBS officers, Lassen was born in Copenhagen and arrived in Great Britain shortly after the beginning of the war. He trained as a Commando, then became a member of the SBS, rising to the rank of major by 1944. Lassen served in the Mediterranean, North Africa, Greece, northwest Europe, the Balkans, and Italy. Having won three Military Crosses for his brave actions in a series of daring operations, Lassen was killed in April 1945 while leading a raid on a German position in Italy. After his death he was awarded the Victoria Cross, Great Britain's highest bravery award.

U.S. NAVY COMBAT DEMOLITION TEAMS

FORMED: 1942-43		STRENGTH: 3,500
AREAS ACTIVE: Western Europe, Pacific		

On June 6, 1944, the Allies launched D-Day—the biggest seaborne invasion in history. The U.S. Navy's specialist naval demolition teams cleared pathways under heavy fire so Allied tanks could go ashore.

Beginnings

The combat demolition teams had their early origins in the costly Allied landings at Gallipoli during World War I, where thousands of British and Australian and New Zealand Army Corps (ANZAC) troops were pinned down and slaughtered by enemy fire. U.S. military leaders later studied the landings to develop new techniques for amphibious warfare.

Operation Torch

For Operation Torch—the Allied landings in North Africa in November 1942—the U.S. Navy employed demolition units as part of its special forces. The six-man teams landed ahead of the main U.S. forces, clearing obstacles such as cables and defensive nets. After this success, U.S. Navy commanders created a specialist force to take on these tasks—the Naval Combat Demolition Units (NCDU).

(Left) Members of an NCDU, having completed their mission, watch Japanese attacks on July 1, 1945, and (inset) an NCDU combat swimmer in action.

Training for D-Day

By early 1944 thousands of Allied troops were stationed in Great Britain, training for D-Day in June. These included 34 NCDU assault teams, each containing 13 men. The scale of the upcoming task was immense—the beaches where the landings were to take place were heavily defended by the Nazis, who had built elaborate obstacles to stop any attempts to stage landings. On some beaches huge steel barricades called "Belgian gates" had been placed in the surf, while mines, fortified machine guns, and mortar positions sat just inland.

Going Ashore

At daybreak on June 6, 1944, D-Day began, and U.S. forces landed on Omaha and Utah beaches. The NCDUs went ashore with the second wave of landings in order to clear 50-foot (15-m) gaps in the beach defenses so that tanks and other vehicles could get onto the beach. Under heavy fire the teams planted their explosives and cleared obstacles. By the end of the day, 13 gaps had been cleared on Omaha beach, at a cost of 31 men killed

IN THE PACIFIC

The Pacific U.S. Navy demolition units were called Underwater Demolition Teams, or UDTs. They were formed in response to the Battle of Tarawa in November 1943, where faulty reconnaissance nearly caused a landing by U.S. Marines to fail. UDTs were active in all the major U.S. actions during the Pacific campaign, including Luzon, Guam, Iwo Jima, Leyte, and Okinawa. In Okinawa nearly 1,000 UDT members provided reconnaissance and demolition support for the invasion.

and 60 wounded. At Utah Beach, 16 pathways were cleared with four killed and 11 wounded. The brave actions of the NCDUs ensured that weapons and reinforcements could keep pouring onto the beaches to allow troops to fight their way inland.

U.S. troops wade ashore on Omaha Beach on D-Day. The work of U.S. NCDUs helped to make the landings possible.

THE U.S. PACIFIC FLEET

ACTIVE:
1941-45

AREAS ACTIVE:
Pacific

STRENGTH:
(1941) 3 aircraft carriers,
9 battleships, 24 cruisers,
80 destroyers, 56 submarines
(1945) 27 aircraft carriers,
8 battleships, and more than
1,150 other vessels

Naval forces were vital to the Allied war effort in the Pacific Ocean. The U.S. Navy's Pacific Fleet bore the brunt of much of the fighting. Here are three critical naval actions fought in the Pacific.

Pearl Harbor

On December 7, 1941, Japanese forces attacked the U.S. naval and air base at Pearl Harbor, Hawaii. Waves of carrier-based planes from the Imperial Japanese First Air Fleet launched a surprise attack at 7:48 a.m. By the end of the day, six U.S. ships, including four battleships, had been sunk, 13 ships damaged, and 188 planes destroyed. More than 2,400 U.S. personnel were killed in the attack. The United States declared war on Japan the next day.

The attack on Pearl Harbor, as seen from a Japanese aircraft. U.S. ships lie at anchor in the foreground.

Battle of Midway

This decisive naval battle took place from June 4–7, 1942, when Japanese forces again attempted to wipe out the U.S. Pacific Fleet. Japanese commanders had planned to ambush U.S. ships near the island of Midway but didn't realize that their secret messages had been intercepted by U.S. code breakers. This allowed the Americans to stage their own ambush. Seven aircraft carriers were involved in this battle—three American and four Japanese. All four Japanese carriers, plus one heavy cruiser, were sunk. The U.S. lost one carrier, the USS *Yorktown*, and one destroyer.

The Japanese cruiser *Mikuma* sinks at the Battle of Midway.

ANZAC SQUADRON

This squadron, containing ships of the Australian, New Zealand, and U.S. navies, was formed in February 1942 to defend northeastern Australia from Japan. The flagship HMAS *Australia* (above), armed with eight 200-mm guns, six antiaircraft guns, and eight torpedo tubes, had a crew of more than 800 and could sail at 35.4 miles (57 km) per hour.

Battle of Leyte Gulf

This epic encounter, believed by many to be the biggest naval battle in history, took place in the Philippines from October 23–26, 1944. In an attempt to starve Japan of vital oil supplies, U.S. forces invaded the island of Leyte on October 20. To oppose them, Japanese commanders sent in almost all of their remaining navy, including nine battleships and four aircraft carriers. Allied forces included 16 aircraft carriers and 12 battleships. The battle ended in a crushing defeat for Japan, which lost four aircraft carriers, three battleships, 10 cruisers, and more than 12,500 men. The Imperial Japanese Navy never sailed again as a large force.

U.S. Navy ships used smokescreens, as shown here, to deter Japanese air attacks during the Battle of Leyte Gulf in 1944.

X-CLASS MIDGET SUBMARINES

FORMED:	STRENGTH:
1943	100 personnel approx.
AREAS ACTIVE: Western Europe, Asia	

Many nations used stealthy midget submarines during the war at sea. One of the most famous was the British X-craft.

A Royal Navy midget submarine being tested in a Scottish loch in 1940.

Mini Raiders

Midget submarines were developed to carry out stealth missions, such as entering an enemy harbor, in order to damage shipping or communications. The vessels were roughly a quarter the length of a normal submarine and carried between one and six crew members. They were designed to be towed to their operating area by a full-sized submarine and towed back to base after the mission was complete.

The cramped interior of an X-craft.

X-Craft

These famous midget submarines were built for the Royal Navy starting in 1943. Crewed by three men—commander, pilot, and engineer—the subs were only 51.2 feet (15.6 m) long. They were powered by a 42 horsepower, four-cylinder diesel engine for running on the surface and an electric motor for traveling while submerged.

X-crafts were normally armed with two high-explosive charges carried on either side of the vessel. In an attack, the crew would drop these underneath the target and set timed fuses to go off.

Operation Source

In September 1943 the Royal Navy launched a daring raid code-named "Operation Source." X-crafts attacked Nazi warships—one of which was the *Bismarck*'s sister battleship *Tirpitz*—which were anchored in a Norwegian fjord. Problems plagued the raid—two of the six X-crafts were lost at sea on the journey north, and two more never made it to their targets. But *X6* and *X7* managed to place their charges, which went off. This caused considerable damage to the *Tirpitz* and kept the ship out of action for months. After the mission, the crews of *X6* and *X7* had to abandon their subs. All were captured and made prisoners of war.

The Nazi battleship *Tirpitz*, shown here, was attacked by X-craft in 1943.

Operation Postage Able

Early in 1944 *X20* undertook a dangerous three-day mission, gathering key information about the Normandy coastline right under the noses of its Nazi defenders. The crew carried out depth soundings and reconnaissance by day and landed divers ashore at night to collect soil samples. This information helped Allied commanders plan the pivotal D-Day landings.

Toward the end of the war, in East Asia, the four-man XE craft was deployed in operations against Japanese forces.

Glossary

aircraft carrier (AIR-kraft KAR-ee-ur)—a large warship used as a floating airbase

Allied forces (AL-lyd FORSS-uhs)—the military forces of Great Britain, its empire and dominions, France and, after 1941, the Soviet Union and the United States

amphibious (am-FIB-ee-uhs)—relating to an attack where vehicles and troops land from the sea

armistice (ARM-iss-tiss)—an agreement between warring sides to stop fighting while a settlement is reached

Axis powers (AK-siss POU-urz)—the military forces of Nazi Germany, Italy, Japan, and some other countries

battle cruiser (bat-uhl KROOZ-uhr)—a large warship with big guns, which is between a cruiser and a battleship in size

battleship (BAT-uhl-ship)—a huge warship

bow (BAU)—the front of a ship

bridge (BRIJ)—the part of a large ship from where it is steered and commanded

capsize (KAP-syz)—when a ship rolls over in the water, usually before sinking

code breaker (KODE BRAYK-uhr)—someone who figures out what an enemy's coded messages mean

Commando (kuh-MAN-doh)—elite special operations troops who are trained to perform dangerous secret missions

convoy (CON-voy)—a large fleet of ships traveling together for protection

corvette (KOR-vet)—a small, fast warship

cruiser (KROOZ-ur)—a medium-sized warship armed with heavy guns

demolition (de-muh-LI-shuhn)—blowing up military targets with explosives

deploy (di-PLOY)—to send into action

depth charge (DEPTH CHAHRJ)—an underwater bomb that explodes at a certain depth

destroyer (di-STROI-ur)—a small, fast warship armed with light guns

dictator (DIK-tay-tuhr)—a leader who wields supreme power to control a country and its people

Holocaust (HOL-uh-kost)—the mass murder of millions of Jews, as well as gypsies, the disabled, homosexuals, and political and religious leaders during World War II

hull (HUHL)—the main body of a ship

intercept (in-tur-SEPT)—to catch up with a target in order to attack it

landing craft (LAND-ing KRAFT)—a flat-bottomed vessel designed to deliver soldiers and vehicles onto a beach

magazine (MAG-uh-zeen)—the part of a warship where ammunition and explosives are stored

Merchant Navy (MUR-chuhnt NAY-vee)—a fleet of ships that goes to sea to carry on trade in goods rather than war

Timeline

1939

September 1 Nazi Germany invades Poland; World War II begins

September 3 Great Britain and France declare war on Germany

September British Expeditionary Force (BEF) sails for France

September Battle of the Atlantic begins; German U-boats sink Allied merchant shipping in the Atlantic Ocean

October HMS *Royal Oak* sunk by a German U-boat at its base in Orkney

1940

April/May Nazi Germany invades Denmark and Norway

May 10 Nazi Germany invades the Netherlands, Belgium, and France

May 26 Operation Dynamo, the Allied evacuation at Dunkirk, begins. Great Britain's Royal Navy and civilian ships play a big part in the evacuation

June 11 Italy joins the war on the Axis side

July 10–October 31 The Battle of Britain—Great Britain's Royal Air Force defeats Nazi Luftwaffe

September 1940–May 1941 Nazi "Blitz" (aerial bombing campaign) on Great Britain

1941

February Hitler sends Rommel's Afrika Korps to North Africa

April Italy and Germany attack Yugoslavia, Greece, and Crete

May 24 Nazi battleship *Bismarck* sinks HMS *Hood*

May 24–27 *Bismarck* is hunted down and sunk by the Royal Navy

June 22 Nazis invade Soviet Union

July Nazi naval "Enigma" code cracked by Allied code breakers

December 7 Japanese attack the U.S. Navy at Pearl Harbor; the United States enters war on Allied side

December Italian forces attack Royal Navy ships with manned torpedoes

navigation (NAV-uh-gay-shuhn)—finding the way at sea

Nazi (NOT-see)—a member of Adolf Hitler's National Socialist Party

neutral (NOO-truhl)—a country is neutral when it doesn't take sides in a war and refuses to fight

obliterate (uh-BLIT-uh-rate)—to destroy or wipe out utterly

obsolete (OB-suh-leet)—a machine that is old and not effective anymore

offensive (uh-FEN-siv)—a planned military attack, often using large forces

pincer movement (PIN-sur MOOV-muhnt)—a military strategy designed to encircle and trap enemy forces

prisoner of war (PRIZ-uhn-ur UHV WAR)—a soldier taken captive and held by enemy forces during a war

reconnaissance (ree-KAH-nuh-suhnss)—finding out information about an enemy's strength by observing or photographing its positions

torpedo (tor-PEE-doh)—an underwater missile dropped from a plane or fired from a submarine in order to sink an enemy ship

U-boat (YOO-boht)—a German submarine; short for *Unterseeboot*

Read More

Benoit, Peter. *The U.S. Navy in World War II*. A True Book. New York: Children's Press, 2015.

Dickmann, Nancy. *The Horror of World War II*. Deadly History. North Mankato, Minn.: Capstone Press, 2018.

Doeden, Matt. *Weapons of World War II*. Weapons of War. North Mankato, Minn.: Capstone Press, 2018.

George, Enzo. *World War II*. Primary Sources in U.S. History. New York: Cavendish Square, 2016.

McGowen, Tom. *The Battle of Midway*. Cornerstones of Freedom. New York: Children's Press, 2018.

Owens, Lisa L. *Attack on Pearl Harbor*. Heroes of World War II. Minneapolis: Lerner Publications, 2019.

Internet Sites

The International Museum of World War II
https://museumofworldwarii.org

The National World War II Museum: New Orleans
https://www.nationalww2museum.org

Smithsonian National Air and Space Museum: World War II
https://airandspace.si.edu/topics/world-war-ii

1942

February 15 Japanese capture Singapore and take 60,000 Allied prisoners

February ANZAC squadron formed

May Battle of Bir Hakeim

June 4–7 U.S. Navy defeats Japanese at key Battle of Midway

June Special Boat Section raids airfields in Crete

November 11 Allies defeat Afrika Korps at El Alamein

November Battle of Stalingrad begins

November 8 Operation Torch begins—U.S. troops land in North Africa; U.S. NCDUs help clear beaches

1943

February 2 Soviet forces defeat Nazi forces at Stalingrad

May 13 Axis forces surrender in North Africa; 275,000 taken prisoner

July 9 Allies invade Sicily

July–August Battle of Kursk

September 3 Allied forces invade Italy at Salerno; Royal Marine Commandos take part in the landings

September 8 Italy surrenders; Nazi Germany now opposes Allied advance through Italy

September Royal Navy X-craft attack German battleship *Tirpitz*

1944

January 22 Allied forces land at Anzio, Italy

January–May Key battle of Monte Cassino in Italy

June 6 D-Day—Allied armies invade Normandy to begin freeing Europe from Nazi forces. RM Commandos and U.S. NCDUs, as well as ships of the Royal Navy, U.S. Navy, and the Free French Navy play key roles

October 23–26 Key naval battle of Leyte Gulf in the Pacific wipes out much of the Imperial Japanese Navy

December 16 Battle of the Bulge begins—Nazi Germany launches its final, unsuccessful offensive in the Ardennes region of France

1945

March 23 Allied forces cross the Rhine River into Germany

April/May Soviet forces close in on Berlin; Hitler commits suicide on April 30 as the German capital falls

May 7 Nazi forces surrender

May 8 VE (Victory in Europe) Day—the war in Europe ends

August 6, August 9 United States drops atomic bombs on Hiroshima and Nagasaki, Japan

August 15 Japan surrenders; VJ (Victory over Japan) Day—the war in the Pacific ends

Index

10th Assault Flotilla, 16–17

ASDIC, 11
atomic bombs, 5
Australia, 4–5, 8, 10–11, 15, 24, 27

Battle of Leyte Gulf, 27
Battle of Midway, 21, 27
Battle of Tarawa, 25
Battle of the Atlantic, 6, 8–9
Battle of the Denmark Strait, 12–13

Canada, 4, 8–10
China, 8, 20
Churchill, Winston, 18
Cockles (folding canoes), 19
code breakers, 13, 27
commandos, 15, 17–19, 22–23
convoys, 8–11
Courtney, Roger, 22
Cousteau, Jacques, 15

D-Day landings, 15, 19, 24–25, 29
depth charges, 10–11

France, 4, 13–16, 19, 25, 29
Free French forces, 14–15
    Léopard, 14
    Montcalm, 15
    Narval, 14
    Richelieu, 15
    Triomphant, 15

Gaulle, Charles de, 14–15
Germany, 4–15, 18–19, 22–23, 25, 28–29
    Bismarck, 12–13, 29
    Prinz Eugen, 12
    Tirpitz, 29
Great Britain, 4–25, 27–29
Greece, 17, 22–23

Hitler, Adolf, 4–5

Imperial Japanese First Air Fleet, 26
Imperial Japanese Navy, 5, 20–21
    Hōshō, 20
    Mikuma, 27
    Yamato, 21
Italy, 4–5, 16–17, 19, 23, 28

Japan, 4–5, 15, 19, 20–21, 23–29

Lassen, Anders, 23

Merchant Navy, 5–6, 8–12, 17
MT assault boats, 17

Nazis, 4–15, 18–19, 22–23, 25, 28–29
Netherlands, 4
New Zealand, 5, 11, 24, 27
North Atlantic, 5–13
Norway, 4, 9, 12–13, 17, 19, 29

Operation Neptune, 15
Operation Overlord, 5
Operation Postage Able, 29
Operation Source, 29
Operation Torch, 24

Pacific, 5, 15, 20–21, 24–27
Pearl Harbor, 4, 20, 26
Pétain, Philippe, 14
Philippines, 27
Prien, Günther, 6

radar, 13, 16, 18, 20
Regia Marina, 16–17
Royal Australian Navy, 5, 10–11, 27
    HMAS, Australia 27
Royal Canadian Navy, 9–11
    HMCS, Haida 10
Royal Marine Commados, 18–19, 22
Royal Navy, 5–13, 16–19, 21–23, 29
    HMS Ark Royal, 13
    HMS Barham, 7
    HMS Dorsetshire, 13
    HMS Hood, 12–13
    HMS Jervis, 17
    HMS King George V, 13
    HMS Prince of Wales, 21
    HMS Queen Elizabeth, 17
    HMS Repulse, 21
    HMS Rodney, 13
    HMS Royal Oak, 6
    HMS Valiant, 17
    HMS Vanoc, 8
    HMS Vansittart, 9
    HMS York, 17
    X-class midgets, 28–29

Scapa Flow, 6
SLC torpedoes, 17
sonar, 11
Soviet Union, 4–5, 9

Special Boat Section, 22–23
submarines, 5–11, 14, 16–17, 19–20, 22–23, 26, 28–29

torpedoes, 6–7, 9–10, 13, 16–17, 20–21, 27
Treaty of Versailles, 4
Truman, Harry, 5

U-boats, 5–11
    Type VII, 7, 10
    U-47, 6
    U-331, 7
    U-971, 10
U.S. Navy, 4–5, 7, 9, 11, 20–21, 23–27
    Combat Demolition Teams, 24–25
    USS Yorktown, 27
    U.S. Pacific Fleet, 4, 26–27
    Underwater Demolition Teams, 25

Vichy France, 14–15

warships, types, 7
World War I, 4, 11, 24